MADRID

THE C

Plaza de
Overlook
and the 1.
(now bein
to arrive in the 1950s – the huge Plaza de
España is a piece of Francoist hubris.

Edificio Carrión
Luis Martínez-Feduchi and Vicente Eced y
Eced brought art deco to the city in 1933 with
this rounded take on the Flatiron Building.
Gran Vía 41

Edificio Telefónica
Ignacio de Cárdenas' 1930 ziggurat might
be US-inspired but it has churrigueresque
elements to its facade and a distinctive clock.
Gran Vía 28

Torre Picasso
Belying its name, the monochrome of this
strict rectangular box points the way to the
Cuatro Torres (see p082) business district.
See p012

Edificio la Unión y el Fénix
The symbol of this insurance company, a
phoenix with its wings spread, perches atop
Modesto López Otero's 1931 art deco tower.
Calle de Alcalá 23

Edificio BBVA Alcalá
Basque sculptor Higinio Basterra cast the
brass and copper chariots that lord over
the former Bank of Bilbao HQ in 1923.
Calle de Alcalá 16

Torres de Colón
Locals know this 1970s twin-towered office
building as *El Enchufe* (The Plug) due to its
bright-green copper upper deck.
Calle Genova 31

INTRODUCTION
THE CHANGING FACE OF THE URBAN SCENE

In the noughties, Madrid went through a cycle of economic growth, urban expansion and creative excitement not seen since La Movida Madrileña in the 1980s. Whereas Barcelona went global when it hosted the 1992 Olympics and has since become saturated with EU émigrés, giving it a superficial veneer of glamour, Madrid's allure runs deeper and its development has been far more organic.

The Euro debt crisis and rising unemployment have been hard on residents, but as locals became more selective in their spending, the city reinvented itself, and a requisite focus on resourcefulness and creativity brought the cream of Spanish talent to the fore. Its social scene continues to thrive and evolve, and although many establishments have pulled down their shutters for the last time, there has been no lack of hip restaurants, bars and clubs to replace them. Now, as always, Madrid's kicking nightlife, immortalised by film director Pedro Almodóvar, suits all budgets and persuasions.

And it is this indomitable spirit, in tandem with the capital's less sybaritic, more highbrow pleasures, of which there are also many (see p032) – and, yes, the low prices – that continue to pull tourists through the award-winning Barajas Airport (see p085) in droves, triggering the opening of design hotels in every district. Madrid, however, has never been a city that feels as if its culture is being stifled by an influx of foreigners. For behind the imperial facade of this vibrant metropolis, you will always find the very soul of Spain.

ESSENTIAL INFO

FACTS, FIGURES AND USEFUL ADDRESSES

TOURIST OFFICE
Centro de Turismo Plaza Mayor
Plaza Mayor 27
T 91 454 4410
www.esmadrid.es

TRANSPORT
Airport transfer
During peak times the metro departs from
T4 every 5 minutes. It takes 12 minutes to
Nuevos Ministerios, from where you can
connect to central Madrid
Car hire
Avis
T 91 548 4204
Metro
Trains run from 6am to 2am
www.metromadrid.es
Taxi
Radio Taxi Asociación Gremial
T 91 447 5180
Travel card
A three-day Abono Transporte Turístico
pass costs €18.40

EMERGENCY SERVICES
Emergencies
T 112
24-hour pharmacy
Antigua Farmacia de la Reina Madre
Calle Mayor 59
T 91 548 0014

EMBASSIES
British Embassy
Paseo de la Castellana 259d
T 91 714 6300
www.ukinspain.fco.gov.uk
US Embassy
Calle de Serrano 75
T 91 587 2200
madrid.usembassy.gov

POSTAL SERVICES
Post office
Paseo del Prado 1
T 91 523 0694
Shipping
UPS
T 90 288 8820

BOOKS
Fortunata and Jacinta by
Benito Pérez Galdós (Penguin)
**Madrid and the Prado:
Art and Architecture** by
Barbara Borngässer (Ullman)
**Remaking Madrid: Culture, Politics
and Identity After Franco** by
Hamilton M Stapell (Palgrave Macmillan)

WEBSITES
Art/Culture
www.madridstreetartproject.com
www.mataderomadrid.org
Newspaper
www.elpais.com

EVENTS
ARCO
www.ifema.es/arcomadrid_06
Estampa Contemporary Art Fair
www.estampa.org

COST OF LIVING
Taxi from Barajas Airport to Centro
€40
Cappuccino
€1.5
Packet of cigarettes
€5
Daily newspaper
€1.50
Bottle of champagne
€50

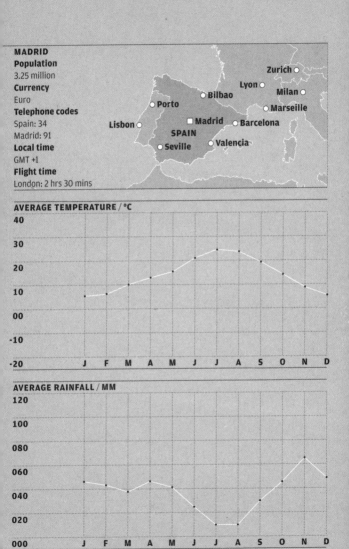

MADRID
Population
3.25 million
Currency
Euro
Telephone codes
Spain: 34
Madrid: 91
Local time
GMT +1
Flight time
London: 2 hrs 30 mins

Zurich ○
Lyon ○   Milan ○
○ Porto   ○ Bilbao   ○ Marseille
Lisbon ○   □ Madrid   ○ Barcelona
SPAIN
○ Seville   ○ Valencia

AVERAGE TEMPERATURE / °C

| 40 |
| 30 |
| 20 |
| 10 |
| 00 |
| -10 |
| -20 |

J F M A M J J A S O N D

AVERAGE RAINFALL / MM

| 120 |
| 100 |
| 080 |
| 060 |
| 040 |
| 020 |
| 000 |

J F M A M J J A S O N D

NEIGHBOURHOODS

THE AREAS YOU NEED TO KNOW AND WHY

To help you navigate the city, we've chosen the most interesting districts (see below and the map inside the back cover) and colour-coded our featured venues, according to their location; those venues that are outside these areas are not coloured.

SALAMANCA

The elegant avenues of this district are home to the upper classes (known locally as *pijos*) and the HQ of national newspaper *ABC*. Gleaming boutiques host global luxury brands alongside high-end local designers. Upmarket eateries such as Otto Madrid (see p056) cater to the elite.

CASTELLANA

Paseo de la Castellana, the city's financial centre, is a multi-lane boulevard lined with skyscrapers (see p082). You'll also find Joan Miró's mural on the Palacio de Congresos (see p072) but most come here to watch the Galácticos play at the Bernabéu (Avenida de Concha Espina 1, T 91 398 4300).

CHUECA/SALESAS

Madrid's gay hub, Chueca has become a playground for all the city's youth, packed with chic restaurants (see p041), funky bars and clubs. Salesas is hailed as Madrid's Soho and its fashion boutiques, and stylish cafés and eateries like Olivia Te Cuida (see p033), draw design-conscious scenesters.

MALASAÑA/TRIBALL

In the 1980s, La Movida Madrileña was born here, and Malasaña is still a mecca for alternative lifestyles, while the shopping strip of Calle de Fuencarral is also a draw. Happening Triball, sandwiched between here and Chueca, is cooler, with gems such as furniture showroom/bar Kikekeller (see p090) hidden down its grubby streets.

CENTRO/LETRAS

The half-moon-shaped Puerta del Sol is a favourite meeting point for locals. A few streets away, the magnificent Plaza Mayor testifies to the might of Spain's former empire. Buzzy, boho Las Letras is steeped in literary history, and the lanes off Calle de las Huertas are unbeatable for tapas.

LAVAPIÉS

Jean Nouvel's bulbous red extension to the Museo Nacional Reina Sofía (see p034) is the gateway to Lavapiés, a working-class area that is starting to gentrify. It's worth a visit for its cutting-edge art galleries and the avant-garde performances held at the Teatro Valle-Inclán (see p086).

LA LATINA

The charming, sloping Plaza de la Paja is a meeting place for Madrid's beautiful people, particularly on Sundays, when lunch at the likes of the nearby Bahiana Club (Calle del Conde 4, T 91 541 6563) is the grand finale to a weekend cavorting around the city's legendary nightlife.

RECOLETOS

Punctuated by the fountains of Apollo, Neptune and Cybele, Paseo del Prado is the western border of the cultural steeplechase (see p032) of refined Recoletos, which is named after a 16th-century monastic order. Those suffering from museum fatigue can find solace in the elegant El Retiro park or a stroll through the Jardín Botánico.

LANDMARKS
THE SHAPE OF THE CITY SKYLINE

It's very likely that your first view of Madrid will be the vaulted roofs and sci-fi spaces of Barajas Airport's Terminal 4 (see p085). It is a fine welcome to today's Spain, where the early-noughties boom found expression in a confident architectural exuberance. The urban landscape expanded thanks to shining new suburbs such as Sanchinarro, and a crop of strikingly modern landmarks were created, including CaixaForum (see p078) by Herzog & de Meuron, and Madrid Matadero (see p036), a vast cultural complex in a former slaughterhouse. Then, of course, there are the Torres KIO (see p014), whose audacious appellation, 'Gateway of Europe', soon started to ring hollow as the leaning portals were dwarfed by a line of four posturing skyscrapers (see p082) just further north.

Declared the capital of Spain in 1561 by King Felipe II, Madrid's grand and austere facades in Centro, Recoletas and Salamanca were bankrolled by imperial gold and silver that poured in from Mexico and Peru. And although the buildings may seem bland in comparison to refined Paris or modernista Barcelona, they are punctuated by architectural gems such as the Palacio Real (Calle de Bailén, T 91 454 8700) and the majesty of Plaza Mayor. The arterial east-west avenue of Gran Vía is lined with ornate blocks that heralded the 20th century, and the statement that is Plaza de España was Franco's 1950s nod to the modernist movement.
For full addresses, see Resources.

Madrid Rio Project

The Manzanares river was reclaimed when the M30 beltway that had flanked it for decades was sent underground. West 8 and MRIO's ambitious landscaping project rejuvenated an area stretching 10km, encompassing parks, plazas, gardens and, as a centrepiece, the two Puentes Cascara (pictured), identical elongated concrete domes connecting Parque de la Arganzuela and Salon de Pinos. Cascara translates as empty shell or fruit peel, yet thanks to more than 100 cables that connect to the steel deck, the bridges evoke the baleen plates of a whale, and the thin-cast aluminium balusters only add to that impression. On the underside of each canopy, photomosaics in recycled glass tiles by artist Daniel Canogar depict locals now floating from one side of the river to the other.

Torre Picasso

When completed by Alas Casariego in 1988, Torre Picasso was the tallest office building in Madrid. Designed by Minoru Yamasaki, the architect of the World Trade Center in New York, the tower has a troubled history of its own – work was suspended in 1984 when the client, an explosives company, suffered financial meltdown and then the architect died. The monolith was devised on a rigorous grid and the vertical lines of the windows are echoed in the landscaping of the plaza in front; the entrance is via a wide arch cut into the two-storey base. It's now owned by Amancio Ortega, the billionaire founder of Spanish fashion brand Zara. At 157m, its height was only surpassed by the Cuatro Torres (see p082) as Castellana reached for the sky in the noughties.
Plaza de Pablo Ruíz Picasso

Círculo de Bellas Artes

The art at Círculo de Bellas Artes, once Madrid's answer to London's ICA, is now more Royal Academy summer show. The ground-floor bar, however, is a 1920s treat of marble busts and chandeliers floating beneath stunning frescoes. The 48m art deco pile was designed in 1919 by Antonio Palacios, who was also responsible for the city's robustly rococo former post office, and is topped by a tower that helps turn the Círculo into such a landmark. The roof terrace is presided over by a magnificent 6m bronze sculpture of Minerva by Juan Luís Vassallo and has a popular outdoor bar, Azotea, and restaurant, Tartan Roof, where local chef Javier Muñoz-Caldero creates his global fusion. Both venues have fine views over Gran Vía and Alcalá. *Calle de Alcalá 42, T 91 360 5400, www.circulobellasartes.com*

Puerta de Europa

Philip Johnson and John Burgee's striking 'Gateway of Europe' comprises two of the most recognisable towers on Madrid's skyline. Completed in 1996, the Torres KIO (they were commissioned by the Kuwait Investment Office and have had various sponsors ever since) are 114m high and lean towards each other at 15-degree angles, making them the first inclined skyscrapers in the world. The glittering structures of granite, steel and glass give an almost surreal, sci-fi impression, looming above the workaday office blocks of Chamartín, and creating a dramatic entrance to the city's glitziest boulevard, Paseo de la Castellana. They frame a statue of José Calvo Sotelo, the politician whose murder in 1936 led to the outbreak of the Spanish Civil War.
Plaza de Castilla

HOTELS

WHERE TO STAY AND WHICH ROOMS TO BOOK

For decades, Madrid's grande dame, Hotel Ritz (Plaza de la Lealtad 5, T 91 701 6767), and belle époque The Westin Palace (Plaza de las Cortes 7, T 91 360 8000), both a stone's throw from the city's centre of gravity, the Prado (see p032), were the only choices for fat cats and celebs. Then, in 1972, the Villa Magna (Paseo de la Castellana 22, T 91 587 1234) arrived to cater for corporate heavyweights.

However, the millennium heralded a building boom as well as a design awakening. Stately 19th-century palaces were spruced up with contemporary interiors that contrasted with their classical facades; the 44 high-ceilinged rooms of Hotel Único (see p030) were executed with perfection, and although the economic crash greatly curtailed development, Urso (see p024) and Only You (see p028) picked up the mantle in 2014. Puerta América (see p020) could be seen as a folly par excellence, but it took some guts to commission a coterie of the world's top architects and designers to leave their mark on one building. Better than that, it has worked.

Increasingly, proprietors are vying to establish their hotels as stand-alone social hotspots and banish the local convention that you're only welcome if you have a room key. There's a lively scene in the eateries and rooftop bars of ME (opposite), Las Letras (see p023), Urban (see p026) and the funky (and great-value) Óscar (Plaza Vázquez de Mella 12, T 91 701 1173), designed by Tomás Alía. *For full addresses and room rates, see Resources.*

ME

Its exterior still looms like a giant wedding cake over the pavement cafés on Plaza de Santa Ana, but the former Reina Victoria hotel's 1920s modernist interior, once a haunt of top matadors, not to mention Ernest Hemingway and Ava Gardner, has been reinvented by architect Keith Hobbs. Of the 192 rooms, the best are the Chic Suite (above) and Suite ME – a two-level haven with a spa and wonderful views. The rooftop bar also offers a fine vista from its gazebos. Gourmet tapas restaurant Ana La Santa (T 91 701 6013), run by Compañia de Lobos (see p041), arrived in 2013, with a modern-rustic vibe by Sandra Tarruella, especially in the Library (overleaf), thanks to its Scandinavian furniture and a stylised bull's head referencing past glories.
Plaza de Santa Ana 14, T 91 701 6000,
www.memadrid.com

Library, Ana La Santa, ME

Silken Puerta América

It began life as a bland conference hotel, but thanks to a visionary approach by Hoteles Silken, Puerta América now doubles as a showcase for some of the 21st century's more renowned designers. Highlights include Marc Newson's high-ceilinged bar, John Pawson's understated lobby (opposite) and Christian Liaigre's smart restaurant; all extraordinary public spaces. Jean Nouvel's take on global glamour pervades the 12th-floor suites, the rooms by Arata Isozaki and David Chipperfield are monochrome and stylish, and Ron Arad's seamless red pod units incorporate a bathroom, storage and a circular bed. Most spectacular of all is Zaha Hadid's Space Club (above), akin to Superman's glacial retreat.
Avenida de América 41, T 91 744 5400, www.hoteles-silken.com

Posada del León de Oro

The cheap-chic concept was extremely popular in Madrid even before the Eurozone crisis, and León de Oro raised the bar when it was renovated in 2010. Located on the same street as most of the city's main tapas bars, this old coaching inn dates to 1893 and is built around a small central courtyard. The redesign was the debut project of Dos Decorando, run by locals Isabel Cortés and Pilar López, who installed a wine bar in the lobby and a glass floor in the restaurant, through which diners can view the old walls of the ancient neighbourhood lying beneath. They also sexed up the smart, minimalist bedrooms, which are spread over three floors. Our favourite is Room 204 (above), which is furnished with modernist classics.
Calle Cava Baja 12, T 91 119 1494, www.posadadelleondeoro.com

Hotel de las Letras

Now part of the Mallorcan chain Grupo Iberostar, Hotel de las Letras occupies an impressive 1917 building by architect Cesáreo Iradier Uriarte, yet after a 2005 renovation by Virginia Figueras and Franco Corada, its stylish interior (lobby, above) couldn't be more contemporary. It has a fine restaurant, Al Trapo (T 91 524 2305), which serves Paco Morales' accessible haute cuisine, a rooftop terrace, Ático las Letras, and a lounge, Bocablo, which has become a stopover for those heading into the centre of town from nearby Chueca. Rooms feature teak and oak panelling, and screen-printed text on the walls. And the literary bent of the 'hotel of letters' doesn't stop there – the ground-floor library has a selection of Spanish classics. *Gran Vía 11, T 91 523 7980, www.hoteldelasletras.com*

Urso

In 2014, Antonio Obrador remodelled José María Mendoza Ussía's elegant 1915 pile, preserving the stained glass, marble floors and beautiful modernista lift. Wallpaper by Iksel decorates the lounge, which has bookcases stocked with first editions, and the light-flooded central atrium, where breakfast is taken on the first floor, while Diego González Ragel's photos show the capital as it was a century ago. Each of the 78 rooms has a view (from large terraces in Suites 401 and 402), there are waterfall showers, and toiletries by The Lab Room, and the minibar is stocked with sweet treats by Caramelos Paco and chocolates by La Duquesita – all local businesses. The basement spa (left), with its 12.5m pool and hydrotherapy stations, is lined with iroko wood, and light streams through sunken windows that frame the original brickwork.
Calle de Mejía Lequerica 8, T 91 444 4458, www.hotelurso.com

Urban

Situated off Puerta del Sol, Urban has brought a touch of avant-garde grandeur to the city centre. The hotel's vaulted steel-and-glass atrium is impressive, despite the nightmare-inducing, sentry-like statues from Papua New Guinea. More sedate original ethnic antiques furnish some of the rooms, whereas in others, such as the Loft Suite (above), there is simply an expert application of natural materials and light. The best views to be had are from the fifth floor, but be sure to master the baffling switches and controls before bedtime. Skip the roof terrace with its tiny pool, but do visit the Glass Bar and Europa Decó restaurant, a haunt of fashionistas and politicos – the Loewe HQ and the congress building are nearby.
Carrera de San Jerónimo 34, T 91 787 7770, www.hotelurban.com

Hospes Madrid

Converted from a handsome 19th-century house, the Hospes has sympathetically preserved many of its features, and it's not difficult to imagine the lobby's former incarnation as the carriage entrance. The 41 spacious rooms are all white with a dash of tangerine or ochre, or perhaps a plum throw. For the most relaxed stay, reserve a Junior Suite (above) under the beamed eaves. Interiors have a playful edge: rococo furniture is painted silver, and oversized baroque lampshades provide contrast in the wood-panelled breakfast room. There's also a small indoor pool. The location near Puerta de Alcalà in the north-west corner of Parque del Retiro is postcard pretty, and the Philippe Starck-designed Ramses restaurant (T 91 435 1666) is next door. *Plaza de la Independencia 3, T 91 432 2911, www.hospes.com*

Only You

The 19th-century residence of the Marquis de Alma has become Chueca's most talked-about boutique hotel, and a destination for the after-work crowd who pack out the cocktail bar (opposite), which is set in a former bookshop, with walnut panelling and original ceiling mouldings, sign and facade. Barcelona designer Lázaro Rosa-Violán has taken an eclectic approach: in the colonial-style lounge, a rhino head is mounted above an open fire; and the lifts are concealed behind a hand-painted tiled wall inspired by Chinese Kangxi porcelain. Each of the 70 rooms is different – some have a pitched beamed ceiling, or a spiral staircase, and the Secret suite (above) has a terrace with great views. Carlos Martín's restaurant is popular for Sunday brunch. *Calle Barquillo 21, T 91 005 2222, www.onlyyouhotels.com*

Hotel Único

María-José Cabré's striking 2011 redesign of this 19th-century mansion features baroque and arabesque touches in the common areas, a 13m-tall Formica and maple sculpture by Jacinto Morós, and the occasional art deco flourish, as in the marble-floored library (pictured). Bijou mosaicked restaurant Ramon Freixa (T 91 781 8262) has two Michelin stars.
Calle de Claudio Coello 67, T 91 781 0173

?4 HOURS

SEE THE BEST OF THE CITY IN JUST ONE DAY

Madrid's museums are world-class, and a whizz through the vast collection at the Museo Nacional del Prado (Calle Ruiz de Alarcón 23, T 91 330 2800) is a must. Head first to the Velázquez rooms to admire his masterpiece of portraiture, *Las Meninas*, and move on to Goya's oeuvre, which ranges from delicate pastoral idylls and subtly satirical royal portraiture to the nightmarish *pinturas negras* that he created after he went deaf. Completing the 'golden triangle' are the Reina Sofía (see p034) and Thyssen-Bornemisza (see p035). If you're in town for the shopping but feel guilty about missing all these highbrow offerings, squeeze in a quick fix at the Centro Cultural Conde Duque (Calle del Conde Duque 11, T 91 480 0401) between retail doses along the same street.

To unwind, Hammam Al Ándalus (Calle de Atocha 14, T 90 233 3334) is a hugely atmospheric bathhouse that dates from the 13th century, when Madrid was part controlled by the Moors. Or picnic by the startling stone columns of Templo de Debod (Calle Ferraz 1), built in Egypt in 200BC and relocated here in 1968 by UNESCO when the Aswan Dam was under construction. Flamenco originates from southern Spain, but many of the great exponents perform in the capital. The oldest *tablao* (literally, floorboard) is Corral de la Morería (Calle de la Morería 17, T 91 365 1137), a restaurant/bar founded in 1956 that puts on two powerful shows each night. *For full addresses, see Resources.*

09.30 Olivia Te Cuida

Madrid's creatives often kickstart their day crammed into this homely café run by Esther Campoy and her husband Fernando Fuentes. The modest 55 sq m space is full of character thanks to vintage furniture, salvaged oak floors and a communal zinc table, where a bunch of fresh flowers and two heavy-duty toasters (powered from on high) take pride of place. Here the regulars gather to toast their *pan rústico* and slather it with olive oil or homemade marmalade and jams to accompany the treats from the extensive breakfast menu, and then linger over the design magazines. The concept is to provide healthy, organic food for time-poor Madrileños, and hence the unusual (for this city) opening hours of 9am to 6pm, except Sundays.
Calle de Santa Teresa 8, T 91 702 0066, www.oliviatecuida.blogspot.com

11.00 Museo Nacional Reina Sofía

Madrid's contemporary art museums are hugely impressive. Begin your cultural quest at Reina Sofía, which opened in 1990 in the remodelled San Carlos hospital, designed in the 18th century by José de Hermosilla and Francisco Sabatini. Jean Nouvel's shiny red 2005 extension formed a new enclosed space (above) in which sits Roy Lichtenstein's *Brushstroke*. Ascend one of the glass elevator towers, designed in conjunction with Ian Ritchie, to the second floor, where Picasso's iconic *Guernica* is the undeniable centrepiece. Other highlights of Spain's artistic canon include work by Miró, Dalí and Chillida, all exhibited in terms of their global context. Afterwards, it's a 10-minute walk to Ana La Santa (see p017) for lunch. Closed Tuesdays.
Calle de Santa Isabel 52, T 91 774 1000, www.museoreinasofia.es

15.00 Museo Thyssen-Bornemisza

When the Spanish state bought Baron Thyssen-Bornemisza's outstanding private art collection for a bargain $350m (on the proviso they would never sell), the Swiss were devastated. But it found a great home in Rafael Moneo's 1992 remodelling of the Villahermosa Palace. A 2004 extension made space for the acquisition of Baroness Thyssen-Bornemisza's collection, and a 2012 overhaul of the museum cafeteria includes a slick terrace (above) with a slatted pergola that overlooks the garden. Hunt down Holbein's portrait of Henry VIII, Rubens' *Venus and Cupid*, Brueghel's *The Garden of Eden* and the expressionists (Kandinsky and Schiele). On the ground floor, 20th-century greats Bacon, Picasso, Pollock and Rothko take centre stage. *Paseo del Prado 8, T 90 276 0511, www.museothyssen.org*

18.00 Matadero Madrid

Luis Bellido's Arganzuela slaughterhouse, a series of limestone and flint pavilions scattered over a 165,000 sq m site, was one of early 20th-century Madrid's most significant buildings. It was reborn as a contemporary arts centre in 2007 by a group of local architects, who carefully preserved its integrity and used recycled materials including polycarbonates and galvanised iron. There's always plenty going on throughout the various spaces. Catch a film in the Cineteca (pictured), which was designed by architects ch+qs; an installation in the refrigeration room; an exhibition in the Central de Diseño; a play in the Naves del Español theatre; and, on summer Fridays and Saturdays, an outdoor concert in the main square. *Paseo de la Chopera 14, T 91 517 7309, www.mataderomadrid.org*

21.30 Platea

The former Carlos III cinema has been
transformed into a foodie mecca, its six
levels presided over by four Spanish chefs
with six Michelin stars between them. On
the first-floor balcony, the star attraction
is Catalan chef Ramon Freixa's Arriba (T 91
219 2305), and its menu spans the nation,
from the fish dough ball *buñuelos* of the
north-eastern beaches to the fried turbot
of Andalucia. Elsewhere, Paco Roncero,
Pepe Solla and Marcos Morán have teamed
up to create a series of concept tapas bars,
specialising in seafood, paella or gazpacho,
and there are also upmarket delis and
cookware stores. Lázaro Rosa-Violán has
beautifully restored Luis Gutiérrez Soto's
1950s extravaganza, adding red leather
banquettes to the balconies. The old stage
now features DJs and live bands, and the
entertainment kicks off around 9.30pm.
Calle Goya 5-7, T 91 577 0025,
www.plateamadrid.com

URBAN LIFE

CAFÉS, RESTAURANTS, BARS AND NIGHTCLUBS

Madrid's restaurants have become more refined in terms of design and ambition, nowhere more so than at the three-Michelin-starred DiverXO (Calle de Padre Damián 23, T 91 570 0766), where David Muñoz's Asian fusion is presented with aplomb. And Nitty Gritty (Calle de Doctor Fleming 51, T 91 434 7333), for example, has a pared-down interior by Mendoza + Simal, and an eclectic menu that visits India and Italy. However, do try the national cuisine, if only to dispel the myth that it is greasy and stodgy. At Sala de Despiece (Calle Ponzano 11, T 91 752 6106), dishes include beef and raspberries 'cooked' by blowtorch. For tapas, head to Huertas or La Latina – the bull's tail and grilled courgette at Viuda de Vacas (Calle del Águila 2, T 91 366 5847) is a rite of passage.

A benefit of the 'crisis' was the death of the soulless gastrobar and the rise of venues with a USP such as Ochenta Grados (Calle de Manuela Malasaña 10, T 91 445 8351), which specialises in low-heat cooking. In TriBall, Clarita (Calle Corredera Baja de San Pablo 19, T 91 522 8070) draws an arty crowd, and La Pescadería (Calle de la Ballesta 32, T 91 523 9051), part of the Lamucca (Calle del Prado 16, T 91 521 0000) empire, does exquisite things with fish. Gourmet markets have also flourished – from the 1916 art nouveau Mercado de San Miguel (Plaza de San Miguel) to the contemporary, organic El Huerto de Lucas (Calle San Lucas 13, T 91 513 5466). *For full addresses, see Resources.*

Bosco de Lobos

Bar Tomate?

Just off touristy Gran Vía, Bosco de Lobos is an oasis of calm in the garden courtyard of the College of Architects, landscaped by Ana Esteve. Within a stand-alone glass box wrapped in a precast cement lattice, this industrial-style restaurant and work space was designed by Sandra Tarruella. The action revolves around the square bar, from where you can watch the chefs work away as you settle in for tapas, or simply sip a *caña* or two. Aside from the small plates, the menu of Italian comfort food includes more interesting dishes such as swordfish carpaccio, and taleggio and black truffle pizza. In fine weather, sit on the terrace in the shade of the birch and chestnut trees. There's also a lounge stocked with architecture books.
Calle Hortaleza 63, T 91 524 9464,
www.encompaniadelobos.com

La Gabinoteca

Architects Ping Pong's tapas den is a pop art labyrinth over two floors, linked by a timber staircase that doubles as a wine rack. Almost every seating area is a talking point, from the booth sunk into a wall or the original Pyrenean chairlift. The *huevo patata y trufa* — egg, potato and truffle cooked in a jam jar — is divine. *Calle Fernández de la Hoz 53, T 91 399 1500, www.lagabinoteca.es*

La Terraza del Casino

If you never got the opportunity to sample the legendary Ferran Adrià's culinary alchemy at elBulli, La Terraza del Casino is a worthy substitute – chef Paco Roncero cut his teeth as one of Adrià's disciples. Despite the experimental menu here, and the striking 2008 refit by Jaime Hayon (see p070), who has teamed Memphis-like pillars with a glossy chequerboard floor, platinum-finished ceramic chandeliers and flowing fabrics, the vibe is traditional: the dress code is strictly jacket and tie for gentlemen. From Roncero's kitchen come dishes such as 'powdered' calamari, hake with seaweed and lilies, and foie gras encased in a white-chocolate shell. The central location gives the summer terrace the added grandeur of excellent city views. *Calle de Alcalá 15, T 91 532 1275, www.casinodemadrid.es*

Casa Mono

Injecting a much-needed dose of fun into the Arguelles district in 2013, Casa Mono has an invitingly ornate, turquoise-painted iron facade, and a similarly retro-inspired interior. In the main room (above), Lázaro Rosa-Violán has clad the walls in green and white tiles, and hung huge iron and glass globe pendants. Other spaces include the mezzanine gin bar, where you can take your pick from 50 labels and 10 tonics.

Bedecked with mismatched chairs, it has a mirrored ceiling festooned with bare light bulbs, which can be rather disorientating after one too many. The kitchen delivers modern takes on classic Spanish recipes: Mono's goat's cheese croquettes deserve all the accolades. There's a buzzy ambience throughout the day, from noon to 2am.
Calle Tutor 37, T 91 452 9552,
www.casamonomadrid.com

Punto MX

Chef Roberto Ruiz's Punto MX became the first European Mexican restaurant to win a Michelin star in 2015. The guacamole is prepared at the table with pestle and mortar, tacos are filled with red tuna or Wagyu beef, and the charbroiled marrow is served in the bone, to be scooped out and wrapped in organic tortillas. It can be hard to secure a table in the basement (opposite), but the Mezcal Lab (above) offers informal dining and plenty of the strong stuff. The venue is characterised by its tiled floors, sourced from Morocco; other nice touches include Utendi's tree-like coat stands with USB ports, and the splashes of Mexican pinks and pulque green in the armchairs, colours that are reflected in the vintage mirror collection.
Calle del General Pardiñas 40,
T 91 402 2226, www.puntomx.es

Dstage

Basque chef Diego Guerrero won two Michelin stars at El Club Allard (T 91 559 0939) and, since going it alone in 2014, has wasted no time collecting another here. In contrast to the OTT interiors often found elsewhere in Madrid, Dstage is pared back. The two floors of exposed brick, concrete and iron, with bare ducts on the ceiling and industrial lighting, centre around a skylit atrium where potted herbs for the kitchen hang on a system of pulleys; the furniture was made-to-measure by a local carpenter. Guerrero is one of the country's most experimental chefs and his molecular creations have included hare tacos and poached-egg desserts. There is no à la carte option; simply two tasting menus of 10 or 13 courses, brought to your table by the chefs themselves. Book in advance as there's only space for 40 at each sitting.
Calle Regueros 8, T 91 702 1586, www.dstageconcept.com

oyster bar
FISHHH!

Luzi Bombón

After the success of Bar Tomate (T 91 702 3870), Barcelona-based Grupo Tragaluz followed it up with the more formal and spacious brasserie Luzi Bombón, in the financial district. Sandra Tarruella used a muted palette of greys and browns, plenty of concrete and wood, and windows facing on to a garden. Custom-made, polished-brass box lights dominate the dining area, and Tarruella also made a feature of the glass-walled kitchen, from where chef Jose Manuel Vila Castro sends out dishes such as tuna tartare with guacamole, and lobster ceviche with *leche de tigre*. If you don't have a reservation, perch at the bar and kick off with succulent Fleur des Eaux oysters. A DJ keeps the vibe lively until 3am on Thursdays, Fridays and Saturdays. *Paseo de la Castellana 35, T 91 702 2736, www.grupotragaluz.com*

TriCiclo

Three is indeed the magic number here at TriCiclo, where a trio of chefs – Javier Goya, Javier Mayor and David Alfonso – have split the menu into three sections, each of which encompasses starters, mains and desserts. The first, Del Mercado, champions fresh produce, be it autumn mushrooms or red Mediterranean prawns; the second, Un Paseo, comprises traditional recipes like oxtail cannelloni; and the third, Un Viaje, looks overseas for inspiration. Dishes can be ordered as half- or third-size (of course) portions, allowing full exploration of the menu. The reclaimed wooden doors and shutters mounted on the walls, furniture sourced from antiques markets, and light fittings made from Vietnamese wicker baskets give the place a rustic, homely feel. *Calle Santa María 28, T 91 024 4798, www.eltriciclo.es*

Le Cabrera

This remains perhaps the hottest gastro-bar in town, due to the cooking of Sergi Arola protégé Benjamin Bensoussan, an extensive list of expertly mixed cocktails and a slick design by Luis Galliussi. The retro basement bar (pictured) gets going from the early evening when the beau monde arrive for post-work drinks.
*Calle de Bárbara de Braganza 2,
T 91 319 9457, www.lecabrera.com*

Magasand

Transformed from a former supermarket by architect Juan Carlos Fernández, this oasis of magazines (maga) and sandwiches (sand) is a temple to relaxation. It exudes a certain Scandinavian cool, courtesy of the furniture – tables from Arper and Matière Grise, wooden chairs in white and peach by Horm, industrial lights by Pols Potten, and some original 1950s pieces including a three-seater sofa by Hans J Wegner. Many of the 'zines on display in the wi-fi-enabled reading zone are not available in Madrileño newsagents. The café/bar is open until 11.30pm. As well as its gourmet creations in bread, it serves salads, crêpes, juices, homemade desserts and cocktails. There's another Magasand branch in Chueca (T 91 319 6825).
Calle Columela 4, T 91 576 8843, www.magasand.com

Dray Martina

Up-and-coming Salesas acquired another feather in its cap with the opening of the shabby-chic Dray Martina in 2013. Versatile design studio Madrid in Love installed a statement wall of salvaged wood arranged in a diagonal pattern and clad the floor and other walls in recycled planks painted white. The vintage furniture was sourced from El Rastro and markets in the south of France, and is a hotchpotch of styles and textures, from leather to bamboo. Light from Constance Guisset's 'Vertigo' lamps bounces off the mirrors, and cacti and flowers provide further warmth. The menu of Mediterranean comfort food throws up the odd surprise combination (octopus with guacamole, hamburgers with mango) and the kitchen remains open all day.
Calle Argensola 7, T 91 081 0056,
www.draymartina.com

Otto Madrid

This 2014 arrival slotted straight into the swanky Salamanca scene, thanks to go-to designer Tomás Alía's sophisticated vision. The entrance is through the buzzy cocktail bar, where a wall of square light fixtures bathe the teak and beige interior in a warm yellow hue. Dine on roast octopus, venison risotto or grilled monkfish in the 'library', where ceramic skulls nestle between the books, or in the VIP area (above), which is wrapped in a Tetris-like study in gold that glints and sparkles at night. The terrace is a summer hangout, and DJ sessions in the blue-backlit tequila bar keep the party in full swing. You'll also find the jet set nearby on Calle de Ayalá, dining on the Asturian cuisine at Ten Con Ten (T 91 575 9254), designed by Alba Hurlé and Alicia Martín. *Paseo de la Castellana 8, T 91 781 0928, www.ottomadrid.com*

Lobby Market

There's no doubting the philosophy of this restaurant/bar. Close-up photography of fresh produce hangs on the exposed brick walls, foliage abounds and floor-to-ceiling shelves are stocked with plants, and jars of spices and oils. Pine sourced from the forests of Soria in northern Spain is also a key feature in architect Julio Touza's scheme. Elsewhere there's a decorative wall of painted planks, and an expansive marble and granite bar, where you can perch to sample a fine selection of hot and cold tapas, available round-the-clock. At lunch or in the evening, take a seat in the dining room for José Ramón Landrin's menu of Spanish and international dishes, such as sea bass ceviche with mango, and roast beef with Périgueux sauce.
Gran Vía 10, T 91 532 6867,
www.lobbymarket.es

Tres Encinas

Since opening in 1967, this celebrated seafood restaurant has been a key fixture on the capital's social scene. After four decades, the owners decided it was time for a refit. Turkish design firm Autoban didn't exactly hold back. Cream-painted art nouveau-style ornamental metalwork lines the ceiling and doors that divide the dining areas, custom-made wall tiles portray a nautical vibe, and the polished parquet flooring plays with perspective. Even more of a statement is the bar, where a block of light frames a display of wine bottles, all high-quality Spanish vintages. Firm favourites from the menu include the seafood croquettes, paella, and local speciality *callos a la madrileña* (tripe). For a quick lunch in the city centre, opt for tapas at the bar. Closed Mondays. *Calle Preciados 33, T 91 521 2207*

La Candelita

This Latin American restaurant and bar in the heart of the gay district offers those occasionally buttoned-up Madrileños an irresistible slice of camp fun. The vibrant walls in acid green, orange and blue, and bamboo, wicker and polished mahogany furnishings set the scene. It could easily have been tacky but designer Ignacio García de Vinuesa – the man behind slick Japanese venue Nikkei 225 (T 91 319 0390) and super-eaterie Zen Market (T 91 457 1873) at the Bernabéu – has pulled off a chic feel. Chef Valerie Iribarren serves treats from Venezuela, Chile, Peru and beyond, including delicious *arepas*. Kick back among the well-heeled clientele in the bar with a pisco sour, or start working your way through the 50 different rums. *Calle Barquillo 30, T 91 523 8553, www.lacandelita.es*

Fuku

It's amazing what owner Hao Wang has achieved with this modern Japanese restaurant in a windowless basement. Olive-coloured walls and banquettes create a cosy feel, there's an illuminated display of haiku sculpture, and the copper mosaic bar is the focal point for chef Yoshie Osanay's flights of fancy. *Calle del Marqués de Villamejor 8, T 91 781 6316, www.fuku.es*

INSIDERS' GUIDE

JAY CUMHUR AND EDGAR CANDEL, DJS/ENTREPRENEURS

Globetrotting DJs The Zombie Kids (www.thezombiekids.es) – Jay Cumhur (opposite, left) and Edgar Candel – release tracks on their own label and run hip burger joint Zombie Bar (Calle del Pez 7, T 91 169 2825) out of their barrio, Malasaña. 'Madrid has so much life. It is full of talented people. There's nowhere quite like it,' says Candel.

A favourite fashion stop is classic Madrid brand Loewe (Gran Vía 8, T 91 522 6815): 'Especially since creative director JW Anderson arrived,' says Cumhur, who likes to accessorise with a rare baseball cap from La Tienda de las Gorras (Calle Corredera Alta de San Pablo 30, T 91 445 1931). A Japanophile, he says that Miyama (Calle de la Flor Baja 5, T 91 540 1386) has the 'best sushi in town', and he's also a fan of TriCiclo (see p051): 'So good it's hard to get a table.'

On an evening out, the duo might start proceedings at Corazón (Calle Valverde 44, T 618 428 175), for its 'cocktail menu and nice vibe', before moving on to Charly's (Calle Jorge Juan 22, T 657 324 700), or perhaps the bar in the Only You hotel (see p029). Always fun is El Fabuloso (Calle de la Estrella 3, T 651 829 373), a retro hangout owned by the 1980s Spanish popstrel Silvia Superstar: 'Rock 'n' roll music and great drinks,' says Candel. The pair keep up with the live-music scene at Mondo Disko (Calle de Alcalá 20, T 91 523 8654) and the Madrid institution Moby Dick (Avenida del Brasil 5, T 91 555 7671): 'It has a killer sound system.'
For full addresses, see Resources.

ART AND DESIGN

GALLERIES, STUDIOS AND PUBLIC SPACES

After almost four decades of stifling dictatorship, the abolition of censorship in 1975 heralded an era of artistic expression, and La Movida Madrileña saw an explosion of creativity as the city raced to catch up with the rest of Europe. Yet the country already had a legacy of great art, of course, thanks to centuries of royals courting painters, who in turn inspired Picasso and Dalí, and it's no surprise that Madrid's major galleries are unmissable. Near the big three (see p032), you'll also find the CaixaForum (see p078) and Real Academía de Bellas Artes (Calle de Alcalá 13, T 91 524 0864), which would be a star attraction in any other city, not least for its 13 Goya paintings. Elsewhere, at Museo Sorolla (Paseo de General Martínez Campos 37, T 91 310 1584), Joaquín Sorolla's canvases are drenched in sunlight in the impressionist's former home.

The parlous state of the economy has hit contemporary design, a luxury that few consumers can now afford. All the more reason to support independents such as EspacioBRUT (see p068), the eco-minded Mad Lab (Calle Abtao 25, T 91 435 9542) and Marre Moerel, who has been producing quirky, organic ceramic lighting and tableware at her Design Studio (Calle de la Luna 19, T 91 523 9059) for the last decade. The art scene has been affected by the crisis too, and with 50 per cent youth unemployment, the most relevant work is no longer in galleries but on the street (opposite). *For full addresses, see Resources.*

Suso33

Acknowledged as the *rey* (king) of graffiti by many of his contemporaries, Barcelona-born Suso33 has been tagging the capital since 1984, and his trademark *Plasta* paint splodge with one staring eye still peers out from shop shutters today. He crossed into the mainstream in the 1990s as institutions including Reina Sofía (see p034) exhibited his work, and has since branched out into performance art – live painting, often with light and audiovisual technology – in more than 50 cities. Shadowy human silhouettes are also a theme, as seen in this formidable *Presencia* mural on an eight-floor block in Tetuán (Plaza del Poeta Leopoldo de Luis, metro stop Estrecho), part of the council's plan to rejuvenate the barrio in which he grew up. It was created from a crane with a can in each hand over two days in 2013. *www.suso33.com*

Parque Juan Carlos I

This former olive grove became Madrid's second-largest park, after Retiro, in 1992, and is a 30-minute drive from the centre, next to Barajas Airport (see p085). José Luis Esteban Penelas and Emilio Esteras Martín's landscaping tour de force sits within a circle, the snaking waterways and paths best appreciated from the air as you land. Within the park are 19 large-scale abstract sculptures. Perched atop a hill is the pillar-box-red donut *Space Mexico* by Andrés Casillas and Margarita García, which looks set to roll away, while Israeli Dani Karavan's *Untitled* (above) combines four olive trees, a tribute to the location's origins, with a series of steel, monastic gateways. The neighbouring 18th-century Parque del Capricho is a lovely picnic spot. *Glorieta Don Juan de Borbón y Battemberg, T 91 721 0079*

EspacioBRUT

Braulio Rodríguez and José Cámara began in El Rastro market in 2009 before moving their refined furniture to this two-floor gallery in Salesas/Chueca. The collection includes sideboards and shelving systems, predominantly constructed from plywood and oak, and distinct for their pastel- or bold-toned lacquers and angled legs, which give the pieces a 1950s feel – the elegant cabinets conjure up Bauhaus modernism and Shaker simplicity. Also on sale here is a fine selection of midcentury classics, from German ceramics to teak tableware, Wegner armchairs and Alvar Aalto lighting, as well as contemporary items. We were drawn to the Scandinavian design by Muuto and washi paper products by the Japanese stationer Siwa. Closed Sundays. *Calle Pelayo 68, T 91 025 8963, www.espaciobrut.com*

BD Madrid

Bocaccio Design (BD) was founded in Barcelona in 1972 by Pep Bonet, Cristian Cirici, Lluís Clotet, Mireia Riera and Oscar Tusquets. It set up in the capital in 1977 and the group expanded to include some of the country's finest designers, such as Rafael Moneo, Javier Mariscal and Elías Torres. The Madrid showroom occupies an 1866 townhouse that retains its original facade, narrow balconies, brick vaults and pine parquet floors, which create a welcoming space. Among the global brands, look out for the Spanish names – we were taken by Nanimarquina's 'Chillida' rugs, Patricia Santos' 'Tree' lamps and the 'Gardenias' range by Jaime Hayon (overleaf). Snap up anything by rising stars Alvaro Catalán and Pedro Feduchi. Closed Sundays.
Calle de Villanueva 5, T 91 435 0627, www.bdmadrid.com

Jaime Hayon

Madrid's enfant terrible Jaime Hayon burst onto the scene in the early noughties. His whimsical, often fantastical furniture and concepts (dinner plates pinned to ceilings, the 'Rocking Hot Dog' chair) now infuse interiors around the world with a nod and a wink, yet his respect for craftsmanship instils finesse, as seen in the fit-out of La Terraza del Casino (see p044). Hayon's playful figurines for Lladró shook up the aesthetic of the porcelain brand, his 'Swivel Catch Chair' (above), for Denmark-based &Tradition, balances cartoon curves with Nordic restraint, and his organic, corner-free scheme for Camper in Tokyo proved that even *Alice in Wonderland*-inspired elements can effuse grace. Hayon is now based in Valencia; his work can be purchased at BD Madrid (see p069). *www.hayonstudio.com*

Muros Tabacalera

During eight days in May 2014, the 10m-high perimeter walls of the Tabacalera, a tobacco factory turned cultural centre, and those down Miguel Servet and Mesón de Paredes, were brought to life by more than 30 artists. An initiative of Madrid Street Art Project, the 100m gallery is refreshed each spring, and crowds gather to watch the murals being created live – above, from left, are panels by Suso33 (see p065), Chylo, Pincho and Rosh333. Elsewhere, local-gone-global Gonzalo Borondo, whose large-scale depictions of the human figure are influenced by Goya and Velázquez, has created a self-portrait. Borondo has several other significant interventions in Madrid, including a scratched-glass ensemble piece in Plaza Mostenses in Malasaña.
Glorieta de Embajadores,
www.murostabacalera.com

Palacio de Congresos
The pièce de résistance of this 1970 congress centre by Pablo Pintado y Riba, on Madrid's grandest avenue, is Joan Miró's fabulous mural. Added in 1980, it comprises 7,056 ceramic pieces and has become a symbol of the city. Miró is also represented at the Museo Arte Público (see p076). *Paseo de la Castellana 99, www.palaciocongresosmadrid.es*

PALACIO DE C

Museo ICO

Housed in a 1970s office block, this act of altruism by Spanish bank ICO opened in 1996. The quarterly exhibitions celebrate architecture, urbanism and photography, recent highlights being a retrospective on Miguel Fisac and Alejandro de la Sota, whose bold modernism brought them into conflict with the tenets of Franco's regime. Displays are often didactic, and include sketches, models and furniture, with tours at weekends. The permanent collection represents the trajectory of 20th-century art in Spain, and includes Picasso's *La Suite Vollard* (100 prints created in the 1930s in exchange for paintings by Renoir and Cézanne), but is almost always out on loan. Check the programme online before visiting, as Museo ICO is not always open. *Calle de Zorrilla 3, T 91 420 1242, www.fundacionico.es*

Museo Arte Público

This flyover, supported by graceful pairs of octagonal pillars, was built in 1968 to connect east and west Madrid. Since 1972 the urban space created underneath and around it has provided a setting for 17 abstract sculptures, each by a Spanish artist, created from the 1930s onwards. The crowd-pleasers are Eduardo Chillida's hanging *Lugar de Encuentros III* (above), dubbed the 'Stranded Mermaid', and Joan Miró's bronze *Mère Ubu*, affectionately known as the 'Penguin'. Four decades of exposure to the elements and the touch of countless hands have given the works a weathered feel, and the shadows cast by the bridge, the roar of the traffic, and the sleeping homeless add to the surrealism. This is no sterile gallery experience.
Paseo de la Castellana 40,
www.madrid.es/museoairelibre

Museo ABC

A relatively recent addition to Madrid's already impressive museum scene, Museo ABC opened in 2010 in the up-and-coming barrio of Conde Duque. It's fair to say that the building itself, a dramatic conversion of a former brewery, is the star. Designed by the Aranguren + Gallegos studio, it has a snowy-white latticed exoskeleton that incorporates the museum, multifunctional areas and restoration workshops, but it is in the café that the architecture reaches its zenith in a long, light-filled space. The collection focuses on the design and illustration of the *ABC* newspaper and, in effect, traces Spain's modern history, in particular the factionalism during the Civil War, when the traditionally conservative paper was seized by Republicans.
Calle de Amaniel 29-31, T 91 758 8379, www.museoabc.es

CaixaForum
Herzog & de Meuron kept the brick shell of this old power station, topped it with cast iron and added Spain's first vertical garden – leaving a striking impression. You enter via its underbelly, up angular steel stairs to seven floors of concrete and oak galleries, where you might catch a study in reportage photography or an exhibition on the artist Miquel Barceló. *Paseo del Prado 36, T 91 330 7300*

ARCHITOUR

A GUIDE TO MADRID'S ICONIC BUILDINGS

Madrid exudes the elegant assurance of a great capital. Grand boulevards converge at neoclassical fountains; the winged lions atop Rafael Moneo's magnificent Estación de Atocha (Plaza de Emperador Carlos V) eyeball the frolicking Greek gods on Ricardo Velázquez Bosco's Ministerio de Agricultura (Paseo de la Infanta Isabel 1); and Paseo del Prado, the stately promenade past the main museums, is sheltered by sycamore and magnolia trees.

However, when it comes to contemporary architecture, there is nothing that comes close to the in-your-face coups of other cities in Spain – the Guggenheim in Bilbao, for example – save perhaps Barajas Airport (see p085). For one thing, there just isn't enough available space in the jam-packed ancient centre. And for another, General Franco wasn't exactly an architecture buff. When Luis Buñuel came to Madrid to shoot *Viridiana* in 1960, he rented an apartment in what he claimed was the city's only skyscraper. There are lots more now – Torres Blancas (Avenida de América 37) arrived soon after in 1968 – but Madrid is stronger at restoring treasures than building new ones. There's the old hospital that is now the Museo Nacional Reina Sofía (see p034), a massive slaughterhouse reimagined as an arts centre (see p036), the 1950s cinema turned gourmet destination Platea (see p038), and Centro Escuelas Pías (see p087), a ruined church reborn as a university library.
For full addresses, see Resources.

Tribunal Constitucional

Dubbed the 'Beehive' or 'Golden Flan', the brutalist HQ of Spain's constitutional court was designed by Catalan Antoni Bonet, co-creator of the 'BKF' chair, with Francisco G Valdés. It opened in 1975, although the Tribunal only moved in six years later. The tapered concrete cylinder, ringed by honey-tinted windows, has offices leading off balconies within its seven-floor atrium; bunkers house the courtroom, library and meeting facilities. In the garden is an olive tree symbolising wisdom, planted by court president Francisco Tomás y Valiente, who was assassinated by Basque separatists ETA in 1996. The structure brings to mind the bulbous columns and circular terraces of Madrid's other standout building from this era, the magnificent Torres Blancas, by Francisco Javier Sáenz de Oiza.
Calle Domenico Scarlatti 6, T 91 550 8000

Cuatro Torres

The city skyline skewed north when these four towers were constructed from 2004 to 2010 on Real Madrid's former training ground at the top of Paseo de la Castellana. At 250m, Torre Bankia (far left; and since rebranded), a stacked-box profile by Foster + Partners, is the tallest building in Spain. Just pipped to that title is the angular Torre Cristal (centre, right), which gets its name from its highly reflective glazing, by Pelli Clarke Pelli. Local architects Carlos Rubio and Enrique Álvarez-Sala's 236m Torre PwC (centre, left) has a double skin that wraps around three fissured sections, and Henry N Cobb's twisted Torre Espacio completes the ensemble. Part of a grand project that was scuppered by the financial downturn, the four behemoths now appear rather stranded – Mansilla + Tuñón's convention centre broke ground in 2009 but is yet to rise above the hoardings.
Paseo de la Castellana

Edificio Mirador

A joint project between Dutch architects MVRDV and Spain's Blanca Lleó, Mirador (which means viewpoint) is successful in many ways. The building itself is a landmark visible for miles around. And, most dramatically, it also has a gaping 13m-high rectangular hole at its centre, within which its occupants can enjoy communal terrace space and great views over the Sierra de Guadarrama. Like a Mondrian painting rising up from the centre of the new, purpose-built northern suburb of Sanchinarro, the Mirador is a 22-storey burst of colour. Known as 'El Donut', the energy-saving edifice is a labyrinth of non-linking corridors and stairways, and nine varieties of flats aimed at 'bringing together diverse social groups with varied lifestyles'. *Calle de Príncesa de Éboli 13, Sanchinarro*

Adolfo Suárez Madrid-Barajas Airport
Richard Rogers' stunning structure has a claim to the title of the world's best-looking airport building. The undulating bamboo awnings of his T4 (above), inaugurated in 2006 and renovated in 2013, subliminally shepherd passengers, irrespective of the language they speak, through check-in and boarding via a colour-coding system. Spread over six floors, the terminal is shaded by the overhanging roof, which is punctuated by a series of apertures, enabling natural light to filter through deep 'canyon' shafts to the lowest levels, thereby minimising energy consumption. Equally impressive is the luggage-sorting system, which requires no handlers and automatically distributes all the cases to the planes from a bomb-proof bunker.
Avenida de la Hispanidad, T 91 321 1000, www.aeropuertomadrid-barajas.com

Teatro Valle-Inclán

Lavapiés, the heart of the Jewish ghetto in the 1400s, has long been a magnet for the city's more colourful denizens, including the militant cigarette girls à la *Carmen* and the *manolos* – lower-class dandies that were such a feature of Madrid in the 1500s. The Teatro Valle-Inclán was charged with revitalising the area when it was built in 2005, yet Lavapiés remains as characterful as ever. However, Paredes Pedrosa's design certainly enlivened the main square and its turn-of-last-century architecture, the boxed volumes making good use of the triangular footprint and its three-cubed frontage shining at night. Inside, the space is unified through spare, sycamore-clad interiors and floor-to-ceiling windows. The theatre puts on an avant-garde programme of works by Spanish playwrights.
Plaza Lavapiés, T 91 505 8801, cdn.mcu.es

Centro Escuelas Pías

For UNED, the Spanish equivalent of the Open University, architect José Ignacio Linazasoro installed a library within the shell of the 17th-century San Fernando church, which was largely destroyed by fire in the Civil War. The introduction of slatted wood and steel creates an ethereal effect, providing sleek synthesis with the existing fabric, and the main reading room, under a cavernous ceiling and halo-like lighting fixtures, takes on a certain monastic aura. The library is only open to the public for 45 minutes on weekdays, at 9.15am and 9pm. Alternatively, the original brickwork can be admired by climbing the geometric staircase (above) to Gau&Cafe (T 91 528 2594), situated on the fourth floor, where the terrace provides great views of the cupola and across the Lavapiés rooftops.
Calle Tribulete 14, T 91 467 5871

SHOPS

THE BEST RETAIL THERAPY AND WHAT TO BUY

The Spanish may not take fashion risks but they love an established label and appreciate tailoring. The flagships of the major national designers like Ágatha Ruíz de la Prada and Adolfo Dominguez are found in La Milla de Oro (The Golden Mile). Also here, Aristocrazy (Calle de Serrano 46, T 91 435 1138) is recommended for jewellery.

TriBall is great for menswear, at stores such as Monkey Garden (Calle del Barco 38, T 91 523 7170), which has a fine edit of US and European brands, and Garcia Madrid (Corredera Baja de San Pablo 26, T 91 522 0521), the showcase of local designer Manuel García. The Plaza Comendadoras area also has plenty to offer, including Sportivo (Calle de Conde Duque 20, T 91 542 5661) for streetwear, Duke (No 18, T 91 542 4849) for shoes, and Mini (Calle del Limón 24, T 91 548 0835) for urban labels. Elsewhere, the streets around Convento de las Salesas Reales are lined with one-off boutiques, from Numero3 (see p092) to Do Design (Calle Fernando VI 13, T 91 310 6217), a café/art gallery stocking fashion, furniture and books.

For homewares, go retro at Vintage 4P (opposite) or LA Studio (Calle Arganzuela 18, T 91 365 7566); find ceramics and lamps at jeweller Helena Rohner (Calle del Almendro 4, T 91 365 7906); and fresh ideas at Stone Designs (Calle de Segovia 10, T 91 540 0336). If you prefer to shop with a G&T in hand, Kikekeller (see p090) transforms into a late-night haunt from Thursdays to Saturdays. *For full addresses, see Resources.*

Vintage 4P

Located near the hectic El Rastro market on Calle de la Ribera de Curtidores, this two-storey treasure trove of quirky vintage European furniture and lighting, displayed against a blank canvas of white walls and pine floors, focuses on the latter half of the 20th century. The turnover here is high, so it's always worth popping in if you happen to be passing. You could pick up a set of black-lacquered Ercol chairs, a 1970s sofa from Sweden or one of owner Juanma Lizana's retro-inspired industrial lights. The only contemporary items on sale are Artefacto's antique plates, cheekily reworked with mash-up designs featuring skeletons or King Kong, and Spanish artist David Martin's cute recycled mini-robots, which have become extremely collectable. *Calle del Bastero 4, T 91 366 5515, www.vintage4p.blogspot.com*

Kikekeller
This delightful showroom is furnished
with Kike Keller and Celia Montoya's
one-off welded furniture, from wrought-
iron chairs to skateboard stools and
pieces made out of scaffolding, as well
as Ángel Tausia's concrete lamps. On
weekends it doubles as a lounge bar, with
a bathroom set in a replica 1920s lift.
Calle Corredera Baja de San Pablo 17,
T 91 522 8767, www.kikekeller.com

Numero3

In this basement boutique you'll find work lockers functioning as a display feature, a lamp made from a vacuum cleaner, and hard hats as decorative elements. It's this fertile imagination that has propelled Concha Díaz del Río to the forefront of the jewellery scene, first with the brand Uno de 50, and now Numero3, a more niche line of rings, necklaces, earrings, bracelets and belts, all handmade in Madrid. The signature pieces, placed in specimen jars, are the chunky wrist cuffs, incorporating buckles, studs and leather. Díaz del Río also designed the brass pendant lights that illuminate the store. One wall is hung with plaques bearing the names of Belgian train stations, meant to inspire Numero3's journey onto the European stage.
Calle de Campoamor 5, T 91 702 3592, www.numero3madrid.com

Ecoalf

The simple white walls, upcycled pine and woodchip, slat pillars and poured concrete floors of Javier Goyeneche's sustainable fashion flagship Ecoalf were designed by Lorenzo Castillo. A street mural by Boa Mistura that states: 'In trash we trust' sets the scene, and inside, everything has been given a second life – rails were once roll bars on military jeeps, and mannequins are made from reconstituted paper. The stylish clothing and accessory range incorporates anything from tyres (in sneaker soles) to coffee grounds (yarn); the Soll Down coat is made from polyester produced from 40 plastic bottles, and recycled wool. As if in an exhibition, jackets are hung in iron box frames, draped with the fishing nets used to create the fabric. Closed Sundays.
Calle Hortaleza 116, T 91 737 4108,
www.ecoalf.com

Isolée

Three years after the runaway success of this streamlined concept store, bar and café in Chueca (T 91 522 8138), the Isolée team brought its one-stop lifestyle shop to Salamanca. There are more than 30 beauty brands in the basement, including unisex range The Lab Room and fragrances by Eight & Bob; the ground floor is given over to fashion, including collaborations like McQueen for Puma; and upstairs are homewares and designer items such as electric bikes, as well as a bookstore, deli and café. The slick, angular, monochrome design by Teresa Sapey, who dreamt up the joyfully colourful parking garage at hotel Puerta América (see p020), centres on a staircase mural of a stylised tree, its branches weaving through the store.
Calle de Claudio Coello 55, T 90 435 6043, www.isolee.com

La Magdalena de Proust

Although Spain is one of Europe's major vegetable and fruit growers, it's rare to find a shop stocking only organic produce. Capitalising on this gap in the market, Laura Martínez and Néstor Calvo opened La Magdalena de Proust in 2012. Its industrial-style ceiling pipes and shelves, recycled ceramic surfaces, fire-engine-red Smeg refrigerators and whitewashed walls give the delicatessen a Japanese flavour, yet chalkboard menus bring back the neighbourhood store feel. The shop sells more than 15 types of bread, seasonal produce from the owners' farm, located 20km from Madrid, and a wealth of natural products, including everything from cava to washing powder. You can also take cooking courses promoting healthy eating.
Calle Regueros 8, T 91 467 3311, www.lamagdalenadeproust.com

ESCAPES

WHERE TO GO IF YOU WANT TO LEAVE TOWN

Slap bang in the centre of Spain, Madrid is the hub of its transport network, so fleeing the capital for a change of rhythm or a couple of days on the coast is simple. The 300kph AVE train, which was introduced as a super-fast link to Seville in 1992, now extends across the country. In the beguiling city of Toledo, ogle El Greco's magnificent *El Expolio* in the cathedral (T 92 522 2241) before lunching on local specialities at Restaurante El Palacete (T 92 522 5375). The architecture of Segovia, hewn from golden sandstone, offers a potted history of Iberia, from its Roman aqueduct to the 16th-century Gothic cathedral, and is a half-hour journey by train.

Other day trips provide a backdrop to the history and culture of the capital. Felipe II's vast palace-monastery, El Escorial (T 91 890 5902) in San Lorenzo, 45km north-west of Madrid, has little of the majesty of similar monomaniacal buildings, but beats them hands-down for artwork. The Bourbon apartments are adorned with beautiful tapestries from cartoons by Goya, and the Museo de Pintura has works by Titian and Ribera. Nearby, a massive cross heralds the tomb of Spain's despot from the recent past, Franco, within the Valle de Los Caídos, which had been built on his orders. Many Republican prisoners of war died constructing this huge brutalist basilica built into the mountain, which was intended to commemorate the Civil War dead of both sides.

For full addresses, see Resources.

Filandón

It's worth making the half-hour drive out to this 2011 opening by the Garcia family, considering the popularity of their fish restaurants O'Pazo (T 91 553 2333) and El Pescador (T 91 402 1290). Designed by Isabel López Vilalta, Filandón's three dining rooms within a granite *finca* can serve up to 400 people a night, yet an air of Zen prevails. Børge Mogensen's beechwood 'J39' chairs and mismatched 'Belloch' seating from Santa & Cole sit around Tom Dixon tables, and there's a roaring, glass-enclosed fire. Outdoor spaces include a glorious courtyard, shaded by maple trees, and a roof terrace. Filandón specialises in seafood, and through the glazed kitchen you'll see lobster, squid and whole fish sizzling on the flame grill. *Carretera Fuencarral-El Pardo, M-612 km1.9, T 91 734 3826, www.filandon.es*

Contemporary Art Centre, Córdoba
Some 300 mosques and palaces were built in Córdoba after the Moorish conquest in the 8th century, and the honeycombed facade of architects Nieto Sobejano's arts centre pays homage to this history, the prefab hexagonal panels referencing the Mezquita. Inside is a maze of concrete and glass, with funnels drawing light into the depths, and an auditorium for film and theatre performances. Nearby, the Museo de Bellas Artes (T 95 710 3659) shows work by important Spanish artists such as Zurbarán, Murillo, Goya and Valdés. Stay at the 16th-century Hospes Palacio del Bailío (T 95 749 8993), for its Roman- and Tuscan-inspired frescoes, a terrace shaded by orange trees, a pool and a plush spa. It takes one hour 40 minutes on the AVE train to reach Córdoba.
Calle Fernández de Córdoba 8

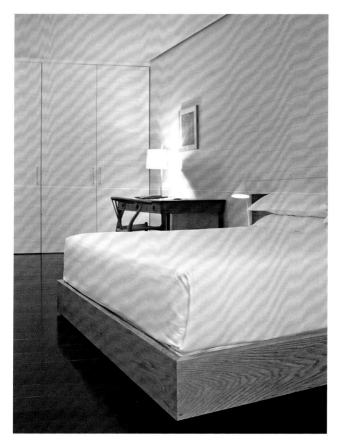

Atrio, Cáceres

The year 1986 was a big one for Cáceres: the Extremadura city (300km from Madrid) became a UNESCO World Heritage Site, for its Roman, Islamic, Gothic and Renaissance architecture; and it gained a gastronomic destination in Atrio. In the historic centre, chef Toño Pérez and sommelier José Polo opened a two-Michelin-starred restaurant and boutique hotel, calling on the Madrid firm Mansilla + Tuñón to create a seamless transition between the two. Pérez's dishes showcase the region's produce, and Polo's cellar is one of Spain's best. The hotel has 14 rooms (Junior Suite 104, above) and a fabulous art collection, which includes original works by Antonio Saura, Antoni Tàpies and, in the breakfast area (opposite), Thomas Demand. *Plaza de San Mateo 1, T 92 724 2928, www.restauranteatrio.com*

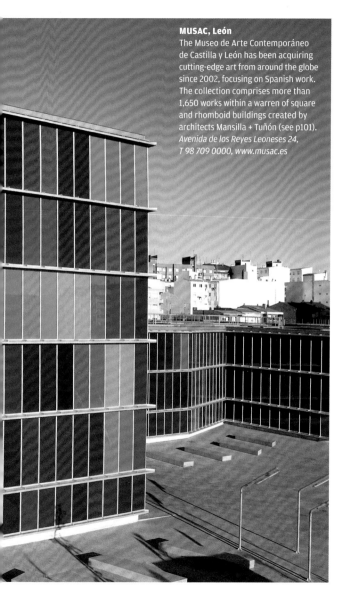

MUSAC, León
The Museo de Arte Contemporáneo de Castilla y León has been acquiring cutting-edge art from around the globe since 2002, focusing on Spanish work. The collection comprises more than 1,650 works within a warren of square and rhomboid buildings created by architects Mansilla + Tuñón (see p101). *Avenida de los Reyes Leoneses 24, T 98 709 0000, www.musac.es*

NOTES
SKETCHES AND MEMOS

Taberna Alhambra -
(Calle de Victoria, 9)
- Gambas a la plancha

Fatigas del Quere
(Calle de la Cruz, 17)
- green olives, anchovies,
croquetas.

Cava Baja (street)
Esteban - Calle Cava Baja, 36
jamon, sherry, pinchos.

La Perejilla - Calle Cava Baja, 25
albondigas

El Escaldon
desserts.

Lamiak - 42 Cava Baja
(bar).
* look for bar ≈ artwork
from Manuel Pastor.

Plaza San Miguel
(market / food court)
try octopus + fried egg.

San Gines.
Pasadizo de San Gines, 5
best churros.

Mercado San Miguel

Bar La Campana
calamari bocadillo.

La Venencia
sherry + mojama.

Bodegas Ricla
tripe, vermut on tap.
boquerones.

Casa del Abuelo
Gambas,
very cool area,
on the corner of a square.

RESOURCES
CITY GUIDE DIRECTORY

A

Adolfo Suárez Madrid-
Barajas Airport 085
Avenida de la Hispanidad
T 91 321 1000
www.aeropuertomadrid-barajas.com

Al Trapo 023
Hotel de las Letras
Gran Vía 11
T 91 524 2305
www.altraporestaurante.com

Ana La Santa 017
ME
Plaza de Santa Ana 14
T 91 701 6013
www.restauranteanalasanta.com

Aristocrazy 088
Calle de Serrano 46
T 91 435 1138
www.aristocrazy.com

Arriba 038
Platea
Calle Goya 5-7
T 91 219 2305
www.plateamadrid.com

B

Bar Tomate 050
Calle de Fernando El Santo 26
T 91 702 3870
www.grupotragaluz.com

BD Madrid 069
Calle de Villanueva 5
T 91 435 0627
www.bdmadrid.com

Bosco de Lobos 041
Calle Hortaleza 63
T 91 524 9464
www.encompaniadelobos.com

C

Le Cabrera 052
Calle de Bárbara de Braganza 2
T 91 319 9457
www.lecabrera.com

CaixaForum 078
Paseo del Prado 36
T 91 330 7300
www.obrasocial.lacaixa.es

La Candelita 059
Calle Barquillo 30
T 91 523 8553
www.lacandelita.es

Casa Mono 045
Calle Tutor 37
T 91 452 9552
www.casamonomadrid.com

Centro Cultural Conde Duque 032
Calle del Conde Duque 11
T 91 480 0401
www.condeduquemadrid.es

Centro Escuelas Pías 087
Calle Tribulete 14
T 91 467 5871

Charly's 062
Calle Jorge Juan 22
T 657 324 700

Círculo de Bellas Artes 013
Calle de Alcalá 42
T 91 360 5400
www.circulobellasartes.com

Clarita 040
Calle Corredera Baja de San Pablo 19
T 91 522 8070
www.claritamadrid.com

El Club Allard 049
Calle de Ferraz 2
T 91 559 0939
www.elcluballard.com

HOTELS
ADDRESSES AND ROOM RATES

Atrio 100
  Room rates:
  double, from €265;
  Junior Suite 104, €385
  Plaza de San Mateo 1
  Cáceres
  T 92 724 2928
  www.restauranteatrio.com

Hospes Madrid 027
  Room rates:
  double, from €610;
  Junior Suite, from €1,160
  Plaza de la Independencia 3
  T 91 432 2911
  www.hospes.com

Hospes Palacio del Bailío 098
  Room rates:
  double, from €510
  Ramírez de las Casas Deza 10-12
  Córdoba
  T 95 749 8993
  www.hospes.com

Hotel de las Letras 023
  Room rates:
  double, from €125
  Gran Vía 11
  T 91 523 7980
  www.hoteldelasletras.com

ME 017
  Room rates:
  double, from €155;
  Chic Suite, from €615;
  Suite ME, €2,500
  Plaza de Santa Ana 14
  T 91 701 6000
  www.memadrid.com

Only You 028
  Room rates:
  double, from €160;
  Secret suite, from €370
  Calle Barquillo 21
  T 91 005 2222
  www.onlyyouhotels.com

Óscar 016
  Room rates:
  double, from €60
  Plaza Vázquez de Mella 12
  T 91 701 1173
  www.oscar.room-matehotels.com

Posada del León de Oro 022
  Room rates:
  double, from €70;
  Room 204, from €120
  Calle Cava Baja 12
  T 91 119 1494
  www.posadadelleondeoro.com

Hotel Ritz 016
  Room rates:
  double, from €645
  Plaza de la Lealtad 5
  T 91 701 6767
  www.ritzmadrid.com

Silken Puerta América 020
  Room rates:
  double, from €90;
  Arata Isozaki suite, from €125;
  David Chipperfield suite, from €125;
  Ron Arad suite, from €125;
  Space Club, from €175
  Avenida de América 41
  T 91 744 5400
  www.hoteles-silken.com

Hotel Único 030
Room rates:
double, from €220
Calle de Claudio Coello 67
T 91 781 0173
www.unicohotelmadrid.com

Urban 026
Room rates:
double, from €600;
Loft Suite, €4,060
Carrera de San Jerónimo 34
T 91 787 7770
www.hotelurban.com

Urso 024
Room rates:
double, from €165;
Suite 401, from €440;
Suite 402, from €440
Calle de Mejía Lequerica 8
T 91 444 4458
www.hotelurso.com

Villa Magna 016
Room rates:
double, from €704
Paseo de la Castellana 22
T 91 587 1234
www.villamagna.es

The Westin Palace 016
Room rates:
double, from €230
Plaza de las Cortes 7
T 91 360 8000
www.westinpalacemadrid.com

WALLPAPER* CITY GUIDES

Executive Editor
Jeremy Case

Authors
Katherine Robinson
Sally Davies
Tara Stevens

Art Editor
Eriko Shimazaki

Photography Editor
Elisa Merlo
Assistant Photography Editor
Nabil Butt

Sub-Editor
Belle Place

Editorial Assistant
Emilee Jane Tombs

Contributors
José Luis Borrachero
Marta Muñoz-Caldero

Interns
Luke Acton
Clara Amzallag
Marta Di Blasi
Juliet Kahne

Production Controller
Sophie Kullmann

Wallpaper*® is a
registered trademark
of IPC Media Limited

First published 2006
Revised and updated
2008, 2011 and 2013
Fifth edition 2015

© Phaidon Press Limited

All prices and venue
information are correct at
time of going to press,
but are subject to change.

Original Design
Loran Stosskopf
Map Illustrator
Russell Bell

Contacts
wcg@phaidon.com
@wallpaperguides

More City Guides
www.phaidon.com/travel

Phaidon Press Limited
Regent's Wharf
All Saints Street
London N1 9PA

Phaidon Press Inc
65 Bleecker Street
New York, NY 10012

Phaidon® is a registered
trademark of Phaidon
Press Limited

www.phaidon.com

A CIP Catalogue record for
this book is available from
the British Library.

Printed in China

ISBN 978 0 7148 6929 2

PHOTOGRAPHERS

Carles Allende
Atrio, p100, p101

Jesús Alonso
Madrid city view,
inside front cover
Madrid Rio Project,
pp010-011
Puerta de Europa,
pp014-015
ME, p017, pp018-019
Posada del León
de Oro, p022
Hotel de las
Letras, p023
Urso, pp024-025
Hospes Madrid, p027
Only You, p028, p029
Hotel Único, pp030-031
Olivia Te Cuida, p033
Museo Nacional Reina
Sofía, p034
Museo Thyssen-
Bornemisza, p035
Matadero Madrid,
pp036-037
Platea, pp038-039
Bosco de Lobos, p041
La Gabinoteca, pp042-043
La Terraza del
Casino, p044
Casa Mono, p045
Punto MX, p046, p047

Dstage, pp048-049
Luzi Bombón, p050
TriCiclo, p051
Le Cabrera, pp052-053
Dray Martina, p055
Otto Madrid, p056
Lobby Market, p057
Tres Encinas, p058
La Candelita, p059
Fuku, pp060-061
Suso33, p065
Parque Juan Carlos I,
pp066-067
EspacioBRUT, p068
BD Madrid, p069
Muros Tabacalera, p071
Museo ICO, pp074-075
Museo Arte Público, p076
CaixaForum, pp078-079
Tribunal Constitucional,
p081
Cuatro Torres, pp082-083
Vintage 4P, p089
Kikekeller, pp090-091
Numero3, p092
Ecoalf, p093
La Magdalena de
Proust, p095
Filandón, p097

Jerónimo Álvarez
Jay Cumhur and Edgar
Candel, p063

Luis Asín
Teatro Valle-Inclán, p086

Gregori Civera
Círculo de Bellas
Artes, p013
Palacio de Congresos,
pp072-073

Roland Halbe
Contemporary Art Centre,
pp098-099

Rob 't Hart
Edificio Mirador, p084

Katsuhisa Kida
Adolfo Suárez Madrid-
Barajas Airport, p085

Ángel Marcos
MUSAC, pp102-103

MADRID

A COLOUR-CODED GUIDE TO THE CITY'S HOT 'HOODS

SALAMANCA
The playground of the upper classes is full of luxury boutiques and swanky restaurants

CASTELLANA
In this northern business district, Madrid's main artery is flanked by office towers

CHUECA/SALESAS
Experience the capital's nightlife in the lively bars and eateries of these vibrant streets

MALASAÑA/TRIBALL
The left-field barrio saw the birth of La Movida Madrileña and is still ahead of the curve

CENTRO/LETRAS
Immerse yourself in the grandeur of imperial history within the magnificent Plaza Mayor

LAVAPIÉS
An artistic quarter that's a draw for its contemporary galleries and progressive theatre

LA LATINA
Do as the fashionable Madrileños do and while away your Sundays in Plaza de la Paja

RECOLETOS
A cultural enclave of museums, fountains and statues, encompassing stately Retiro park

For a full description of each neighbourhood, see the Introduction.
Featured venues are colour-coded, according to the district in which they are located.